The Vampire Library

Vampire History
and Lore

STUART A. KALLEN

ReferencePoint
Press®

San Diego, CA

About the Author

Stuart A. Kallen is a prolific author who has written more than 250 nonfiction books for children and young adults over the past 20 years. His books have covered countless aspects of human history, culture, and science, from the building of the pyramids to the music of the twenty-first century. Some of his recent titles include *Crop Circles*, *Werewolves*, and *Toxic Waste*.

©2011 ReferencePoint Press, Inc.

For more information, contact:
ReferencePoint Press, Inc.
PO Box 27779
San Diego, CA 92198
www.ReferencePointPress.com

Picture credits:
Cover: Fortean Picture Library
AP Images: 22, 52
Fortean Picture Library: 40, 69
iStockphoto.com: 32
North Wind: 12, 42
Photofest: 6, 8, 72, 74

Series design and book layout:
Amy Stirnkorb

LIBRARY OF CONGRESS CATALOGING-IN-PUBLICATION DATA

Kallen, Stuart A., 1955-
  Vampire history and lore / by Stuart A. Kallen.
     p. cm. -- (Vampire library)
  Includes bibliographical references and index.
  ISBN-13: 978-1-60152-132-3 (hardback)
  ISBN-10: 1-60152-132-4 (hardback)
  1. Vampires. I. Title.
  BF1556.K34 2011
  398'.45--dc22
                                                          2010005866

Contents

The Kiss That Kills

In 1928 English occult researcher Montague Summers wrote: "In all the darkest pages of the malign supernatural there is no more terrible tradition than that of the Vampire, a pariah even among demons. Foul are his ravages; gruesome and seemingly barbaric are the ancient and approved methods by which folk must rid themselves of this hideous pest."[1] As Summers's words demonstrate, long before vampires appeared in books, films, and on television as beautiful, misunderstood creatures, they were considered the most vile and repulsive monsters that ever walked the earth.

While people in centuries past might have longed for the vampire's immortality, it was understood that vampirism came with a terrible price. A reanimated corpse that rises from a grave can only survive by plunging its fangs deep into the flesh of a living being and draining its blood. In the dark, foreboding forests of ancient Europe, where vampire legends were strongest, no sane person would have wished for the vampire's kiss—not even if it meant living forever.

Foul Vampires in Europe

As early as A.D. 950, the Arab chronicler Ibn Masudi described eastern European pagans drinking the blood of sacrificed animals to attain immortality. By the eleventh century those who performed this act, along with other antireligious deeds such as worshipping idols or performing black magic, were referred to as vampires. In 1047 the word first appeared in print when an unnamed Russian priest described Prince Vladimir Yaroslavovich from Great Novgorod as "Upir' Likhyi," which roughly translates from old Russian to mean "wicked or foul vampire." The Russian words used by the priest had parallels in other Slavic languages. In Serbian the words translated as *vampoir*, and the Hungarian *vámpír* was spelled *vampir* in German. The word *vampire* first appeared in English around the mid-1700s.

However the word was spelled, the 1700s are remembered as the era of the vampire epidemic. During this time, thousands of vampires were said to be loose in the European countryside. Terror swept through villages, and countless corpses were exhumed so that stakes could be driven through their hearts—a common method for killing vampires at the time. A typical description appeared in the 1733 *Dissertation on Serbian Vampires*, written by German scholar John Heinrich Zopfius:

> Vampires issue forth from their graves in the night, attack people sleeping quietly in their beds, suck out all the blood from their bodies and destroy them. They beset men, women and children alike, sparing neither age nor sex. Those who are under the fatal malignity of their influence complain of suffocation and

In the 1931 horror film Dracula, *actor Bela Lugosi (pictured) portrayed the central character as suave, sophisticated, and menacing. Lugosi's portrayal solidified in the public mind the image created 30-plus years earlier by author Bram Stoker.*

a total deficiency of spirits, after which they soon expire. Some who, when at the point of death, have been asked if they can tell what is causing their decease, reply that such and such persons, lately dead, have risen from the tomb to torment and torture them.[2]

From Hideous to Hunk

For reasons unknown the plague of vampirism ended in Europe around the late eighteenth century. But like the immortal creatures that rose from the dead, vampire stories returned with a vengeance in the late 1800s. Bram Stoker's *Dracula* became a best seller in 1897 and set off a new wave of interest in the undead, but refashioned for a new age. Count Dracula, the leading character of Stoker's story, was suave, sophisticated, and rich. He lived as an aristocrat in a castle and used his considerable charm to mask his evil intentions.

Dracula and other Dracula-like characters were kept alive throughout the twentieth century and into the twenty-first century by countless movies, books, and television shows. The 1931 horror film *Dracula* introduced the blood-drinking count to millions of viewers for the first time. Newspapers reported that when *Dracula* premiered at the Roxy Theater in February 1931, dozens of audience members were so frightened they fainted. Dracula also lived on in silly comedies such as 1979's *Love at First Bite*. And in books the vampire was transformed again and again. In 1976 novelist Anne Rice created Lestat, a tall, handsome blood drinker with long blond hair and complex emotions. In the Southern Vampire Mysteries series of novels by Charlaine Harris, vampires are often portrayed as sexy hunks. And in

In Interview with the Vampire, *author Anne Rice created the vampire Lestat—a tall, handsome blood drinker with long hair and complex emotions. Actor Tom Cruise played Lestat (pictured) in the movie version of Rice's book.*

the Twilight series by American author Stephenie Meyer, the permanently 17-year-old vampire Edward Cullen is a loving, romantic vampire who would never harm any human beings.

Legends of the ancient bloodsucker originated in the poverty and ignorance of rural villages. And the primal fear of blood-drinking immortal vampires is as old as human history. But with billions of dollars to be made in books, TV shows, and films, it is a sure bet that vampire stories will be around for many years to come.

Chapter 1

A History Written in Blood

In December 2002 panic swept through the African nation of Malawi. Rumors spread that vampires in that famine-stricken country were attacking people for their blood. Villagers barricaded themselves in their homes. Farmers were so fearful of vampires that they refused to work in the fields to harvest desperately needed food. The vampires were believed to be Westerners who were working with the government to gather human blood in exchange for food aid.

About a dozen people—men, women, and children—complained to authorities and journalists that they had been bitten by vampires. As a result, vigilantes began attacking suspicious-looking strangers. One man accused of working for vampires was stoned to death in the Mulanje district. In the village of Thyolo, three European Catholic priests suspected of gathering blood for sale were seriously beaten and jailed. The situation was so bad that President Bakili Muluzi had to dispatch cabinet members to south Malawi to calm what he called "malicious and irresponsible"[3] rumors.

Fear Still Exists

The idea that vampires might really exist may seem strange to most people today, yet the events in Malawi show that fears of blood-drinking monsters still exist in some parts of the globe. Vampire legends abound, from the bloodsucking witches of Tlaxcala, Mexico, to the mosquito-like monster *aswang* of the Philippines. Many of the undead fiends appear as beautiful women who fly through the night like birds before attacking their victims. Other walking dead, called revenants, are debonair and handsome men.

Sometimes bloodsuckers, like the Australian *yara-ma-yha-who*, are so hideous they almost defy description. This creature has a small body, a huge head, and octopus-like suckers on its hands and feet. The *yara-ma-yha-who* drops from fig trees and drinks a victim's blood, only to return later and eat the corpse whole. Then it regurgitates its disgusting dinner, which comes back to life as a furry bush creature.

Ekimmu and the House of Darkness

Whatever a vampire's characteristics or feeding habits, most trace their lineage back to the oldest known bloodsucker in recorded history. More than 3,600 years ago, the great civilization known as Babylonia was founded in present-day Iraq. Babylonians developed the concepts of astronomy, mathematics, medicine, and philosophy as they are known today. The Babylonians also believed that when a person died, he or she descended underground to a place called the House of Darkness. There the dead would spend eternity in a horrid, gloomy world ruled by the god Irkalla. Unless their living relatives were generous enough to leave meat and drinking water on their graves, underground dwellers were forced to eat dust and mud when they were hungry.

The
Yara-ma-yha-who

In Australia the Aboriginal people speak of a vampire-like creature called the *yara-ma-yha-who*. This creature looks like a small, red man, about 4 feet (1.2m) tall with an enormous head and a mouth with no teeth. The tips of the creature's fingers and toes are covered with suckers, like an octopus.

Yara-ma-yha-who live in the tops of fig trees, where they wait for prey. When an unsuspecting traveler comes to rest in the shade of the tree, the *yara-ma-yha-who* jumps down. It attaches its suckers to the victim and drains the blood from the body. This does not kill the person but leaves him or her disoriented. The vampire then takes a nap, but when it awakens it sucks the still-living victim's body into its gaping mouth. Sometimes the *yara-ma-yha-who* will regurgitate its meal, and the prey will emerge alive. However, the victim will be shorter than before and will soon grow hair all over his or her body and become a furry creature of the forest.

People who died of natural causes were trapped forever in the House of Darkness. But bloodsucking demons called *ekimmu* suffered what was thought to be a worse fate. Their corpses could not enter the House of Darkness. Instead *ekimmus* wandered through the world, able to see old friends and relatives but never able to partake of the joy of living again.

The word *ekimmu* means "that which was snatched away," a label that was applied to someone who met an untimely death through murder or accident. These people were primarily thought to have died either of drowning or from dehydration in the hot, barren desert. However, that changed as the centuries passed. A dead person might return as an *ekimmu* if he or she were not given a proper funeral and buried according to religious traditions or had no relatives to tend the grave. In *The Vampire: His Kith and Kin*, Montague Summers quotes an ancient Babylonian incantation that describes the conditions by which an *ekimmu* is made:

> He that lieth in a ditch...
> He that no grave covereth...
> He that lieth uncovered,
> Whose head is uncovered with dust,...
> The hungry man who in his hunger hath not smelt the smell of food,
> He whom the bank of a river hath made to perish,
> He that hath died in the desert or marshes,
> He that a storm hath overwhelmed in the desert,...
> He that hath posterity and he that hath none.[4]

Whatever their manner of death, *ekimmu* revenants had many traits in common with modern vampires. They had superhuman strength and could move through the air like wind, smoke, or dust. *Ekimmus* often appeared as walking corpses—thin, extremely pale, covered with scabs and sores, and perpetually thirsty for blood. The creatures also had the ability to shape-shift; that is, assume the appearance of old men, animals, or winged demons.

Because *ekimmu*s were refused entry into the House of Darkness, they were mean tempered and extremely violent. To find victims, the monsters haunted remote valleys and deserts. When unwary travelers passed, the *ekimmus* fed on their blood and life energy, or soul. Rather than kill, the unseen *ekimmu* might attach itself to the skin like a leech and feed off its prey for months. During this time of torment, an *ekimmu* might act like a poltergeist, a noisy ghost who wrecks furniture, breaks pots and dishes, and wreaks general havoc. Once a house was infested by an *ekimmu*, it was nearly impossible to make it leave. The victim eventually turned into a drained husk of a human who withered away until death.

Ashanti Vampires

The *ekimmu* is one of the first supernatural vampires described in recorded history. And the creature's vile characteristics lived on in Africa where bloodsuckers were said to fly through the air and drain the lifeblood from victims.

African vampires were associated with witches called *obayifo* said to be living among the Ashanti people in Ghana. Male or female *obayifo* lived incognito, blending in with the neighbors. However, when night fell, the *obayifo* were said to shape-shift into balls of bright phosphorescent light that traveled rapidly from village to village. The *obayifo* could attack anyone and drink his or her blood, but the evil creatures preferred children. *Obayifo* also sucked the juices from fruits and vegetables, rendering them inedible. This was done on a large scale so entire crops or fruit orchards were destroyed, visiting misery and hunger on the local population.

In past centuries bloodsucking witches were thought to be living in almost every Ashanti community. However, the malevolent monsters had several traits that gave them away. An *obayifo* was said to have shifty eyes with a penetrating gaze. And the witch often demonstrated an unusual interest in eating, especially raw meat.

Ashanti lore describes another vampire-like monster called the *asasabonsam*. This creature was human in appearance except for its long, iron teeth and hooked feet. It purportedly lived in the deepest forests, where few people traveled. To catch its prey, the *asasabonsam* perched on tree branches and dangled its long legs over a trail. When a traveler passed by, the *asasabonsam* used its hooked feet to snare the victim. Once it trapped a traveler, the vampire drank his or her blood before disposing of the drained corpse on the trail.

Vampire Witches

East of Ghana, in Nigeria, the Ibo people tell tales of witches that engaged in vampirism as well as cannibalism and necrophagy, or feeding on the flesh of the dead. These bloodsucking witches flew invisibly through the air and met with demons to plan attacks on innocent victims. The vampire witches entered houses through holes in the roof.

Strange as It Sounds...

The mortal enemy of the Ashanti *obayifo* was a shaman, or witch doctor, called an *okomfo*, who used magic spells to destroy the evil bloodsucker.

While the victim slept, the vampire entered the body through the stomach. Once inside the body, the vampire witches could wind around vital organs such as the heart, liver, and lungs. The victim might die immediately or suffer a long, painful death. In 1906 Rhodesian army major Arthur Glyn Leonard wrote that death was accomplished by "gradually sucking the blood of the victim through some supernatural and invisible means, the effect of which on the victim is imperceptible to others."[5]

Legend has it that once the vampire witches obtained human blood, it was used to create a special magical brew for casting spells. In 1937 anthropologist M.J. Field wrote about the process in *Religion and Medicine of the Ga People*:

> When the witches meet they are believed to gather 'round a pot called baisea. . . . The pot is often supposed to contain the "blood" of the victims. The "blood" appears to ordinary eyes as mere water, but it contains the vitality of the victim. And though the victim has lost none of his tangible blood and bleeds in the normal way when cut, the essential properties of his blood have been "sucked" and transformed to the pot to be drunk by the witches.[6]

In some parts of Africa, the belief in vampire witches continues to this day, and many common illnesses such as ulcers, cancer, tuberculosis, and heart disease are blamed on bloodsucking witches. Oftentimes there are accusations of vampirism when a healthy person falls ill. Older, unmarried women are most often blamed for sucking out a person's vitality.

Punishing Vampires

Fears of vampire witches were so great that in past centuries those accused of vampirism were hideously punished before being killed. The tongue was pulled out and pinned to the chin with a large thorn in order to prevent the perpetrator from uttering a final curse against his or her executioners. The accused witch was then impaled on a sharp stake, which caused a slow, painful death. Once the heart stopped beating, the body was burned and the severed head was left in the forest to be eaten by scavengers.

The torture of accused vampire witches was halted in the early twentieth century. At that time more humane practices were put into place. When a suspected vampire witch was detained, the authorities would try to convince her to change her ways. This created quite a mess, however, as Field writes: "Occasionally, when a witch is arrested, confesses, and consents to reform, she begins by vomiting all the 'blood' she has ever sucked."[7]

The Flying *Loogaroo*

In the late seventeenth century, millions of West Africans were forced into slavery and shipped to the New World. Common beliefs about vampire witches were carried by the West Africans to Haiti, Trinidad, and Grenada in the Caribbean, and to Suriname in South America.

In Haiti people speak of a *loogaroo*, an old woman who, like the Ashanti *obayifo*, can shed her skin and fly through the night as a blue ball of light. The *loogaroo* has many supernatural powers, but they were granted to her by the devil so she must pay a price. Every night her satanic master demands a delivery of fresh human blood. Because the *loogaroo* does not want to provide her own blood, she must

The Sound of Leathery Wings

In the thirteenth century a folktale from the Middle East described the problems that afflicted a traveler after he was attacked by an *ekimmu* disguised as an old man. The story begins when a wealthy wayfarer takes pity on a sad old man standing by the banks of a stream. The old man is afraid to wade through the rushing water, so the traveler offers to carry him across on his back. But as the two reach the middle of the stream, the old man tightens his withered arms around the traveler's throat. In a low hiss, the old man says that he is an ekimmu and he will remain on the wayfarer's back for the rest of his life. The tale continues:

> The man returned home with the creature on his back,

where it would rest invisibly for the remainder of his days. He had formerly been quite prosperous but, over the years, that prosperity began to slip away and he found himself . . . on the verge of becoming a beggar. This was put down to the *ekimmu* . . . [which] acted exactly like a vampire. Eventually the man died and, as he did so, there was the sound of leathery wings flying away, although nothing was seen. The *ekimmu* had invisibly departed.

Quoted in Bob Curran, *Vampires: A Field Guide to the Creatures That Stalk the Night*. Franklin Lakes, NJ: New Page, 2005, pp. 32–33.

obtain it from others by swooping into homes and obtaining it from sleeping victims. After she has delivered her bowl of gore, she crawls back into her skin. In 1928 Montague Summers wrote about the Haitian vampires:

> Even today visitors to Haiti have been called out of the house late at night by servants to see the loogaroos, and their attention is directed to any solitary light which happens to flash through the darkness. . . . Until dawn the loogaroos are at work, and any [native] who feels tired and languid upon awakening will swear that the vampire has sucked his blood.[8]

Potential victims can protect themselves from the *loogaroo* because the monster has one peculiar trait. When the creature sees sand, it must stop to count all the grains. Therefore, superstitious people leave a pile of sand near their doors and windows. When the *loogaroo* comes calling, it will first stop to count all the grains of sand. This process takes so long, the sun comes up before the creature can collect the blood demanded by the devil.

Anyone wishing to kill a *loogaroo* must find her skin. It is said she folds it up neatly and hides it in the bushes near a silk-cotton tree, also called a devil tree or jumbie tree. Vampire hunters search for the skin at night. When they find it, they pound it with a pestle, or grinding implement, and cover it with salt and pepper. When the *loogaroo* tries to climb back into her skin, she perishes in wretched agony.

Summers writes that widespread fear of the *loogaroo* occasionally provided cover for those wishing to commit petty crimes. He claims that it was common for a burglar wishing to steal the valuable cocoa pods from a farmer's tree to wave a "lantern fashioned from an empty dried calabash [gourd] cut to imitate grotesque and gargoyled features [of the loogaroo], and lighted by a candle set in a socket."[9] From a distance, the gourd looks frighteningly like a vampire witch and prevents honest citizens from stopping the cocoa thieves.

The Man-Bat and Blood Toad

All manner of bloodsucking beasts appear in the creation story of the Maya of Guatemala and southern Mexico. The story, called the *Popol Vuh*, tells of a vampire-like deity with frightening features called Camazotz. Camazotz is a vicious man-bat that attacks its victims with its razor-sharp nose, teeth, and claws and drinks their blood. It lives in a cave called the Bat House located in the Maya underworld. In the *Popol Vuh* twin brothers enter the underworld to avenge the death of their father, and they are first attacked by vampire bats and then by the man-bat Camazotz. Because of this legend, the Maya traditionally avoided caves where vampire bats resided. But the angry creature was a popular subject for ancient Maya artists and architects. Some of these works, dating from around the seventh century, can still be seen today.

In the fourteenth century the Aztec culture came to dominate the region of Mexico north of the former Maya territories, and they too had a story that featured frightening vampire-like deities. The Aztec believed that a goddess named Tlaltecuhtli was a sea monster who lived before creation. Two deities, Quetzalcoatl and Tezcatlipoca, wanted to create the earth but were terrified when they first saw Tlaltecuhtli. She appeared as a massive toad with fangs and jaws on her face, knees, and elbows, all dripping blood.

Believing the earth could not survive with this bloody toad on the loose, Quetzalcoatl and Tezcatlipoca ripped her in half. One part of Tlaltecuhtli was thrown in the air to create the stars and sky, and the other half was used to make the rock and soil of earth. Her eyes became springs and rivers, and her hair became the trees. This act did not kill the bloody toad, but it made her want to drink human blood.

The Aztec practiced human sacrifice to placate Tlaltecuhtli's awesome thirst for blood. During this ritual the heart of the sacrificial victim was pulled out of the chest while the person was still alive. The heart was then placed in a stone box carved with pictures of the blood toad goddess.

The ancient Aztecs practiced human sacrifice to placate the goddess Tlaltecuhtli, who thirsted for human blood. Two skeletons found at an ancient Aztec settlement in Mexico provide proof of Aztec rituals involving human sacrifice.

This was done in the belief that Tlaltecuhtli thrived on hearts ripped from the bodies of the sacrificial victims.

Several other gruesome Aztec goddesses are associated with vampirism and human sacrifice. Cihuacoatl was depicted with two fang-like knives on her forehead above a gaping mouth always open to receive victims. However, like many vampires the world over, Cihuacoatl could transform into a beautiful woman. Using her charms to seduce strong young men, the goddess killed her victims and drank their blood. In order to appease her bloodlust, the Aztec sacrificed prisoners to Cihuacoatl on a regular basis.

Bloodsucking Witchcraft

Some of the most terrifying Aztec blood-drinking deities originated as mortal women who died in childbirth. As a result, they returned as goddesses, called *cihuateteo*, and wandered the earth at night attacking children, either paralyzing or killing them. In hopes of preventing assaults, Aztec women left food at busy crossroads. This was done in the belief that the *cihuateteo* would stuff themselves with food until morning, when they would be killed by the sunlight.

After the Spanish conquered the Aztec in the sixteenth century, Christianity replaced native beliefs. However, fears of vampire goddesses lived on for centuries in the form of shape-shifting, bloodsucking female witches called *tlahuelpuchi*. The *tlahuelpuchi* practiced bloodsucking witchcraft and used supernatural powers to transform themselves into a wide variety of animals. A *tlahuelpuchi* might appear as the family cat or dog or as a flea on the pet's back. Ants in the yard might really be bloodsucking witches, or the women might shape-shift into barnyard animals such as donkeys, cows, and chickens. The bloodsuckers could also fly through the air as ducks, buzzards, and crows, but for unknown reasons they most often appeared as turkeys. Anthropologists collecting accounts of *tlahuelpuchi* sightings between 1959 and 1966 found that 75 percent of all incidents of bloodsucking witchcraft involved vampires disguised as turkeys.

Unlike typical European vampires, *tlahuelpuchi* could not pass their curse to others through spells or bites. That is because bloodsucking witches were born with their evil powers, which did not present themselves until they reached puberty. At that point *tlahuelpuchi* underwent a transformation called *espanto*, or the losing of the soul, which took place over a period of three days. After that, *tlahuelpuchi* could shape-shift while developing a voracious and uncontrollable desire to drink human blood, especially from babies.

According to legend, bloodsucking witches went on their gruesome missions at night, but first they had to perform the ritual that transformed them into animals. A fire was built with plant material believed to have magical, transformational powers, such as capulin wood, copal, century plant roots, and dry zoapatle leaves. Once the flames were blazing, the witch chanted a magical spell, walked over the burning coals three times, and finally sat upon the fire. This separated the lower legs and feet from the body and turned the *tlahuelpuchi* into a dog. The bloodsucker then went out into the night and transformed once again, this time into a turkey, chicken, or other animal. If the vampire witch did not find a victim by daylight, she would die. But if human blood was drunk, the *tlahuelpuchi* returned home, sat on the fire again, and shifted back to human form.

Born with a Curse

While *tlahuelpuchi* were believed to be common in Mexican society, they were rarely mentioned in conversation. Those who were related to the bloodsucking witches were gripped by a great sense of shame and hopelessness and did not speak of their troubles. Average citizens were afraid to expose the *tlahuelpuchi* they might have known about. This was based on the fear that the witches could hear everything said about them and would instantly kill a person who exposed them.

While people were frightened of bloodsucking witches, there was an unusual ambivalence about them, since it was believed that *tlahuelpuchi* did not choose their fate. Instead they were born evil and had no control over their powers. This gave rise to the saying "tlahuelpuchis are born with a curse that neither God nor the devil can erase."[10]

Vampire-like beings have been a part of human culture dating back thousands of years. The creatures appear in countless gruesome shapes in stories told around the globe. With their ceaseless thirst for blood, the vampire demons have haunted the world and left a ghastly legacy from the Middle East and Africa to South America, Mexico, and beyond.

Chapter 2

Spirits Walking by Night

Long ago in ancient Greece, people believed the best way to kill a vampire was to drive a stake through its heart and cut off its head. It was also said that once the head was removed from the body, it should be boiled in vinegar. This would ensure that the corpse could not rise again as a vampire. This morbid ritual is one of many vampire stories and rituals that appear in the mythology of the ancient Greeks.

Greek legends from the first millennium B.C. describe three vampire-like creatures. The *strige* or *strix*, after the Latin word for screech owl, was both a vampire and a witch. Using magic to turn herself into a flying night demon, she swooped down on babies and children, drank their blood, and left them for dead. Unlike vampires of later times, the *strix* was not a dead human come back to life but a creature that transformed from a human into a monstrous beast.

One of the most renowned *strix* from classical literature appears in the comedic play *Pseudolus*, or *The Cheat*, by Roman playwright Titus Maccius Plautus. In the play, written around 191 B.C., a chef is describing the horrible food prepared by unskilled, inferior cooks. These rogues use ingredients so foul that the food is like eating a *strix*. The cook states, "These fellows, when they cook dinners . . .

season them, not with seasonings, but with vampyre owls which eat out the bowels of the guests while still alive."[11]

Lamia and Hobgoblins

There was nothing funny about another type of ancient Greek vampire, the *lamia*. These were women whose lower bodies were snake-like and malformed. Their feet were mismatched and extremely odd. One human-like foot was made of brass, and the other foot resembled the hoof of a donkey, ox, or goat. Although horrible to gaze upon, the *lamia* could transform themselves into beautiful women who used their charms to ensnare innocent young men.

The hideous monsters were named after Lamia, a mortal woman who was the queen of Libya and mistress to the Greek god Zeus. The queen had several children with Zeus, but they were murdered by his jealous wife, the goddess Hera. Lamia did not have the power to exact revenge upon the goddess, so she lashed out at the human race, killing children by drinking their blood. This transformed Lamia into a ghastly creature who spawned legions of bloodsucking *lamia*.

One of the most famous stories featuring a *lamia*, *Life of Apollonius*, was written by the Athenian author Philostratus in the first century A.D. The story is narrated by Apollonius, who meets a handsome student named Menippus, 25 years of age. Although Menippus is endowed with good judgment, he is smitten with a "foreign woman, who was good-looking and extremely dainty, and said that she was rich."[12] The woman declared her love for Menippus, saying, "you will hear my voice as I sing to you, and you shall have wine such as you never before drank, and there will be no rival to disturb you; and we two beautiful beings will live together."[13]

After spending the night with the mysterious stranger,

The Corpse of the Wizard-King

Ireland is not known as a home for vampires. But in the fifth century, the remote north Derry region was said to be haunted by an evil, blood-sucking wizard named Abhartach. Historical accounts of Abhartach say he was a cruel chieftain who lorded over a population too terrified to kill him. The frightened peasants persuaded another chieftain, Cathán, to murder Abhartach. After his death, legend holds that Abhartach was buried standing up in an isolated grave. But the corpse of the wizard-king rose from the grave the following day. Standing before the petrified populace, Abhartach demanded they open their veins and fill a giant bowl with their blood so that he could sustain his loathsome corpse. Cathán killed Abhartach again, and he was reburied, but the king returned the following day, demanding another bowl of blood.

The perplexed Cathán consulted with a local holy man named John to find out why Abhartach would not stay dead. John told him, "Abhartach is not really alive. Through his devilish arts he has become one of the neamh-mhairbh [the undead]. Moreover, he is a dearg-dililat, a drinker of human blood. He cannot actually be slain but he can be restrained." John told Cathán to kill the wizard with a sword made from yew wood, bury him upside down, and place heavy stones upon the grave. This worked, and Abhartach never bothered the living again.

Quoted in Bob Curran, "Abhartach the Vampire," O'Kane Genealogy, 2003. www.ocathain.com.

Menippus agrees to marry her in the morning. However, Apollonius arrives before the wedding can take place and warns Menippus: "I say, this fine bride is one of the vampires, that is to say of those beings whom the many regard as lamias and hobgoblins. These beings fall in love, and they are devoted to the delights of Aphrodite [love], but especially to the flesh of human beings, and they decoy with such delights those whom they mean to devour in their feasts."[14]

After this statement, the bride-to-be yells at Apollonius and calls him a liar. But Apollonius is proved to be correct when the beautiful decorations and fine food and wine the bride had provided for the wedding turn out to be illusions. Finally, she begins to weep and admits that she is indeed a vampire and was fattening up Menippus to eat him. As Apollonius states, "It was her habit to feed upon young and beautiful bodies, because their blood is pure and strong."[15]

Throats Full of Blood

When Roman culture replaced that of classical Greece in the first centuries A.D., the alluring characteristics of the vampire faded as well. Instead Roman legends described two kinds of vampires, both frightening to behold. The Greek *strix* became the Roman *striga vie*, or a living, bloodsucking witch, recognizable by her full, red lips and bright red face. This creature did not prey upon her victims personally, but sent her soul out to kill babies and innocent young men and women. Another type of Roman vampire, called the *strigoi mort*, was a dead thing that drank the lifeblood of its victims. The *strigoi mort* vampires could be seen cavorting in the moonlight, dancing hand in hand with *striga vie* witches.

Eventually, the living and dead vampires of Rome merged into a single creature, a witch called *strigoi*. Like the *strix*, the witch could transform itself into a carnivorous bird. The Roman poet Ovid described the *strigoi* in the first-century poem *Fasti*: "They fly by night and look for children without nurses, snatch them from their cradles and defile their bodies. They are said to lacerate the entrails of infants with their beaks, and they have their throats full of the blood they have drunk."[16]

According to Ovid, there were steps that could be taken to prevent children from being defiled in this terrible manner. As protection, parents would spray their doorsteps with an herbal mixture made of water and the flowers of the arbutus tree, which was thought to be a strigoi repellent. A spell was then cast in which the petitioner shook the bloody entrails of a pig and chanted: "Birds of the night, spare the entrails of the boy. For a small boy a small victim falls. Take heart for heart, I pray, entrails for entrails. This life we give you in place of a better one."[17] The ritual was complete when a white thorn branch was placed in the window of the home.

"He Casteth a Glamour"

In the early years of the first millennium A.D., the Romans conquered much of the European continent and Great Britain. As the Roman legions rolled north, east, and west of present-day Italy, the ancient belief in blood-drinking witches followed them. In 380, when Roman Catholicism became the official religion of the Roman Empire, the bloodlust of witches and vampires became closely associated with the evils of Satan. This may be seen in a fourth-century collection of religious laws, or *nomocanon*, produced by the Greek Orthodox Church that discusses vampires called *vrykolakas*:

> It is impossible that a dead man should become a *vrykolakas*, unless it be by the power of the

The Roman poet Ovid wrote of various methods that could be used to protect children from the blood-drinking child snatchers known as strigoi. One method involved spraying doorsteps with a mixture of water and the flowers of the arbutus tree (pictured).

Devil who, wishing to mock and delude some . . . and so very often at night he casteth a glamour whereby men imagine that the dead man whom they knew formerly, appears and holds [conversations] with them. . . . At other times they may behold him in the road, yea, even in the highway walking to and fro or standing still, and what is more than this he is even said to have strangled men and to have slain them.[18]

This ancient holy writ goes on to say that when such a vampire is discovered, there is a "riot and a racket" as townsfolk hurry to the cemetery to exhume the wandering corpse. They find that the corpse seems to be alive, "the dead man—one who has long been dead and buried—appears to them to have flesh and blood. So they collect together a mighty pile of dry wood and set fire to this and lay the body upon it so that they burn it and they destroy it all together."[19]

The Infernal Hellhound

Although the church described vampires and publicized methods to kill them, it did so while condemning such beliefs. The official church policy was that vampires were a pagan superstition and belief in blood drinkers should be discouraged. By the eighth century the church took strong measures against vampire legends. The Saxons, who ruled parts of present-day Germany and Great

Britain, decreed the death penalty for anyone who professed to believe in vampires or who defiled a corpse thought to be a vampire. Despite this law, accounts of vampires continued long after the Saxon empire crumbled. Some of the most detailed accounts from the medieval period were written by English historian William of Newbury (or Newburgh) around 1196.

William reports that while it may have defied common sense, vampire molestations were quite common in England. In addition, there were so many reports of vampires that they could not all be written down in one book. William writes:

> It would not be easy to believe that the corpses of the dead should sally . . . from their graves, and should wander about to the terror or destruction of the living, and again return to the tomb, which of its own accord spontaneously opened to receive them, did not frequent examples, occurring in our own times, suffice to establish this fact, to the truth of which there is abundant testimony. . . . Moreover, were I to write down all the instances of this kind which I have ascertained to have befallen in our times, the undertaking would be beyond measure laborious and troublesome.[20]

Unlike the vampires from earlier times, the English revenants did not drink blood. Instead they beat people black and blue and spread disease with their breath. William writes of one case, reported by a respected monk in Anantis, near York, in which a man suspected his wife of being unfaithful to him. He told her he was going on a long trip but returned to his house and climbed up in the rafters to hide near the ceiling. When a young neighbor boy came to visit his wife, the man, in a fit of jealousy, fell from the rafters and crashed onto the floor. The jealous man died the next day from injuries sustained in the fall, but terrible troubles followed. According to William:

> A Christian burial, indeed, he received . . . but it did not much benefit him: for issuing, by the handiwork of Satan, from his grave at night-time, and pursued by a pack of dogs with horrible barkings, he wandered through the courts and around the houses while all men made fast their doors, and did not dare to go on any errand whatever from the beginning of the night until the sunrise, for fear of meeting and being beaten black and blue by this vagrant monster. But those precautions were of no avail; for the atmosphere, poisoned by the vagaries of this foul carcass, filled every house with disease and death by its pestiferous breath.[21]

So great was the fear of this vagrant monster that almost everyone moved away from Anantis. However, on a Palm Sunday two brothers whose father had died at the hands of the revenant decided to destroy the wandering corpse. The young men grabbed several spades and went to the cemetery. They had just begun to dig when they found the corpse "swollen to an enormous corpulence, with its countenance beyond measure turgid and suffused with blood; while the [burial shroud] in which it had been wrapped appeared nearly torn to pieces." When the men began beating the

Strange as It Sounds...

In ancient times, pagans supplemented their meager diets by consuming animal blood either raw or mixed with grain and vegetables into patties called relish cakes.

corpse with their shovels, blood flowed from the body as if it were alive, with such a stream as if it were "a leech filled with the blood of many persons."[22]

The men dragged the corpse to a large pile of wood and, using their blunt spades, removed the heart from the body and tore it to bits. The wood was lit on fire, the vampire was burned to ashes, and peace was restored in the village. According to William, "When that infernal hell-hound had thus been destroyed, the pestilence which was rife among the people ceased, as if the air, which had been corrupted by the contagious motions of the dreadful corpse, were already purified by the fire which had consumed it."[23]

Things That Go Bump in the Night

Blood-engorged hellhounds terrified medieval Europeans long after William of Newbury died in 1198. By the sixteenth century vampire lore was so popular that religious experts such as Swiss Protestant theologian Lewes Lavater found it necessary to discourage folk beliefs in the undead. In his 1572 book *Of Ghosts and Spirits Walking by Night*, Lavater stated that some vampire sightings were the hallucinations of people who were simply fearful of "things that go bump in the night."[24] Lavater also pointed out that drunken young men sometimes pulled pranks to scare their neighbors, dressing in rags and smearing their faces with mud to look like dead bodies.

More serious hoaxes were perpetrated by rogue priests who exploited public fears of vampires. The priests convinced parishioners that they could provide defense from vampire attacks through a magical process called necromancy. This purportedly allowed the priests to speak to the dead and convince them not to bother certain people. However, priests charged large sums for such services, allowing a few necromancers to grow quite wealthy. As Lavater writes, "There have been in all ages certain priests, which practicing strange devices, and giving themselves to necromancy, have bewitched foolish men that highly esteem them, to the end that they might thereby increase their riches, and follow their lustful pleasures."[25]

Enemies of Humankind

After discussing corrupt priests and troublemaking hoaxers, Lavater did acknowledge that authentic vampires could "appear in the shape of a man recently killed, in a pleasing or horrible form . . . and will threaten [people] and use vile language."[26] Like many religious authorities, Lavater wanted to make sure that people understood the difference between real and fake vampires. This was in keeping with a medieval tradition that exploited vampire fears to make sure people attended church. As parapsychologist Rosemary Ellen Guiley explains in *The Complete Vampire Companion*, "The church stressed that the unconverted and unrepentant would become vampires after death."[27]

Fears of vampirism were also used as a type of social control to prevent criminal behavior. For example, it was commonly believed that murderers, rapists, robbers, and prostitutes would become vampires after death. In eastern Europe vampirism was also associated with heavy alcohol consumption. According to Guiley, "It was believed that the addiction to drinking would not be stopped by death and that the restless soul would turn to drinking blood as a substitute."[28]

Those who dabbled in the dark arts of witchcraft and wizardry were also destined to become vampires, according to stories from medieval Europe. In rural Romania living witches and warlocks, called *moroii*, have long been said to thrive on animal or human blood. Known as living vampires, these sorcerers sell their souls to Satan in order to gain magical powers. The *moroii* are easily identified by their appearance. Males are extremely pale and hairless, whereas females have plump, red lips and exceptionally red faces. *Moroii* are shape-shifters, able to change into many types of animals, including birds, wolves, and bugs. After taking animal form they would wreak havoc on their enemies, spreading disease and causing accidents and disasters.

Because *moroii* were humans, they could be killed. However, this might turn them into something worse—a true vampire. Bob Curran, a professor of Celtic history, describes these deadly creatures as "physical corpses that knew no rest and were motivated solely by evil. All humanity appeared to have left them and they were now implacable enemies of humankind."[29]

Vlad the Impaler

One of the most notorious kings in European history, Vlad Dracula III, is remembered as a ruthless vampire. *Dracula* means "son of the dragon," which also translates to "son of the devil." But Dracula, who ruled Wallachia, a principality bordering Transylvania, Romania, was widely known as Vlad the Impaler. This nickname is derived from his preferred method of disposing of enemies—impaling them on long, wooden stakes while they slowly bled to death over many hours or days.

Dracula ruled Wallachia between 1448 and 1476. His reign of terror began in 1457 when his army invaded Transylvania, pillaged the countryside, and set villages, castles, and farms aflame. Prisoners were burned alive or taken back to Dracula's castle, where they were shoved down onto long, upright stakes that passed through their entire bodies.

Strange as It Sounds...

In Romanian folklore, bloodsucking witches called *strigoi* are considered close relatives of werewolves and grotesquely evil creatures called goblins.

Bloodbaths with Báthory

Countess Elizabeth Báthory, born in Hungary in 1560, was a member of a powerful noble family whose relatives ruled various parts of eastern Europe for more than three centuries. She is also one of the most famous real vampires in recorded history.

Báthory was described as brilliant, beautiful, and intelligent, with the ability to read and write in four languages. However, she had a violent temper, and as she grew older she became obsessed with preserving her beauty at any cost. After consulting with witches, demonologists, alchemists, and other sorcerers, Báthory concluded that blood from young virgins would keep her looking young forever. At the age of 44, she ordered her chief torturer, a dwarf named Johannes Ujvary, to cut open a young girl and drain her blood into a huge vat. The countess bathed in the warm blood and declared it a perfect beauty tonic. During the five years that followed, the countess's servants kidnapped beautiful female peasants and drained their blood for Báthory's beauty baths. However, in 1610 the countess was arrested. During her trial it was revealed she had killed 650 victims and bathed in their blood. As punishment she was confined to a room in her torture chamber, where she survived for three years. After Báthory's death, the records of her trial were sealed so that scandal would not be brought upon the royal house of Báthory.

Dracula's most notorious crime took place on April 2, 1459, when his army burned the city of Brasov to the ground. Hundreds of citizens were marched to a huge circle on a hill and impaled. As they writhed in pain and screamed for mercy, Dracula sat at a table placed in the center of the circle, feasting, dining, and laughing with his lieutenants. About 40 years after the event, the scene was depicted on a German woodcut that shows the writhing masses of impaled men and women with bulging eyes and gaping mouths. Dracula sits at a dinner table while a man stands before him chopping up a corpse with an ax. Thousands of paper pamphlets emblazoned with the woodcut circulated throughout Europe and established Dracula's reputation as a vampire. As the inscription reads: "Here begins the very cruel and frightening story about a wild bloodthirsty man, voivode [governor] Dracula. How he impaled people, roasted them and boiled them in a kettle, and how he skinned them and hacked them into pieces. . . . and many other horrible things are written in this tract and also in which land he had ruled."[30]

Dracula's crimes continued unabated, and in 1460 he committed an atrocity that was unmatched in Europe up to that time. Upon raiding the town of Amlas, Dracula ordered 20,000 to 30,000 men, women, and children impaled on a single night. Two years later the tyrant's army rounded up 23,000 Turkish soldiers and marched them to Dracula's castle. All were impaled in a single day as Dracula watched with pleasure. By the time Dracula was captured and imprisoned in 1462, as many as 100,000 people had been impaled, burned, boiled, nailed, decapitated, hanged, skinned, or buried alive—all at the behest of Dracula.

Vlad Dracula the Impaler died in 1476, but more than 400 years after his demise, the bloody Romanian king provided inspiration for the lead character in Bram Stoker's novel *Dracula*. And in doing so, Dracula took his place in history alongside female vampires, gory witches, and other bloodsucking monsters that trace their lineage back to the horrible beasts that haunted the Greeks, Romans, and British for thousands of years.

In this famous woodcut, villagers impaled on sharp wooden stakes suffer a gruesome death while the corpses of others are chopped into pieces and prepared for roasting. In the middle of it all, Vlad Dracula feasts.

Chapter 3

A Plague of Vampires

Beginning in the mid-1300s, the Black Death, or bubonic plague, killed tens of millions of people. The plague continued to haunt Europe for more than 300 years. In the seventeenth century alone, the Black Death killed more than 10 million people, and carts piled high with dead bodies were rolled through the streets of nearly every village, town, and city. At the end of the 1600s, another type of epidemic swept across the land. Its appearance was as inexplicable as the Black Death, and it caused nearly as much panic. It was the plague of vampires that began in eastern Europe and left its mark from southern Italy to northern England.

The plague of vampires took place at a time when the printed word was making a large impact on society and more people were reading than ever before. Publishers of pamphlets, newsletters, newspapers, and inexpensive books were competing for customers, and nothing attracted an audience faster than news about vampires. As a result, the historical record from the late 1600s to the late 1700s is full of detailed accounts of vampires written by scientists, scholars, and religious leaders. The reports stoked public fears while detailing vampire characteristics and attacks, as well as methods for hunting and killing bloodsuckers.

Vampires Appear After Lunch

Public fascination with vampires in the early 1700s can be traced to the French newspaper *Mercure gallant*. In 1694 the paper reported a story that took place in an unnamed town in which "vampires appeared after lunch and stayed until midnight, sucking the blood of people and cattle in great abundance. They sucked through the mouth [and] nose but mainly through the ears. They say that the vampires had a sort of hunger that made them chew even their shrouds in the grave."[31]

Few vampire stories of the time depict vampires as sucking blood through the ears or nose, but the chewing of burial shrouds was a common feature in these stories. In eighteenth-century Europe, cadavers were wrapped in white cotton or linen cloths called winding sheets or burial shrouds. If the body of a suspected vampire was exhumed, the shroud was often masticated, or chewed. In 1725 German author Michaël Ranft wrote an entire book on the subject called *Of the Dead Who Masticate in Their Graves*. Ranft stated that corpses chew not only their winding sheets but even their own flesh. To prevent the ghastly gnawing, in some parts of Germany the dead were buried with dirt under their chins, stones packed into their mouths, or handkerchiefs tightly wound around their throats.

Ranft gives several examples of the dead in Moravia who masticated in their graves. One unnamed woman, disinterred in the sixteenth century, was said to have nibbled on her own entrails. In another case, a dead man gulped down the winding sheet of a woman buried next to him. In 1746 Dom Augustine Calmet, a French Bible scholar of the Benedictine order, discussed Ranft's stories in his book, *The Phantom World: The History and Philosophy of Spirits,*

OPPOSITE: Workers in seventeenth-century England bury the bodies of those killed by bubonic plague. Another plague descended on England and other parts of Europe around this time: a plague of vampires.

Apparitions, Etc. Calmet wrote of accounts by villagers of horrific sounds during shroud chewing, and cadavers are "heard to eat like pigs, with a certain low cry, and as if growling and grunting."[32]

He Looked as When Alive

Stories about the dead chewing like pigs in their graves were common throughout Moravia, Hungary, eastern Prussia, and Serbia in the 1720s. And Calmet's description of the alleged vampire Peter Plogojovitz (also spelled Plogojowitz) added fuel to the flames of the vampire hysteria. Plogojovitz died in Kisolova, Serbia, in 1725. Ten weeks after his burial, he began appearing in the bedrooms of villagers, seizing them by the neck, and choking them to death. Within 8 days, 9 people were said to have been killed by the dead man. Terrified townsfolk begged authorities in the Hungarian emperor's army to stop the attacks. An officer who did not believe in vampires sent some soldiers to exhume the corpse of Plogojovitz. The men expected to find a pale cadaver that had been decomposing for nearly 3 months. Calmet describes what the men discovered instead:

> [Having] caused Peter Plogojovitz to be exhumed, they found that his body exhaled no bad smell; that he looked as when alive, except the tip of the nose; that his hair and beard had grown, and instead of his nails which had fallen off, new ones had come; that under his cuticle, which appeared whitish, there was a new skin, which looked healthy, and of a natural color; his feet and hands were as whole as could be desired in a living man.

They remarked also in his mouth some fresh blood, which these people believed that this vampire had sucked from the men whose death he had occasioned.[33]

Upon discovering this plump corpse, the townsfolk quickly drove a sharpened stake through the heart of Plogojovitz. This caused a large quantity of crimson blood to shoot from the wound as well as from the nose and mouth. The startled peasants dragged Plogojovitz's body to a pile of burning wood and reduced his corpse to ashes, after which they were bothered no more.

An Arch-Vampire

Peasants were fearful of vampires like Plogojovitz because they believed vampirism was a contagious disease like the bubonic plague. Victims of bloodsuckers could therefore "catch" the disease and become vampires themselves. Driven by such fears, the plague of vampirism spread like wildfire. The epidemic reached such proportions that in 1731 Holy Roman emperor Charles VI sent vampire investigators to Belgrade, Serbia, which was part of his empire. The investigators included a clergyman and several army doctors, including military surgeon Johann Flückinger. In the preamble of the official report concerning the investigation, Flückinger wrote, "Having heard from various quarters that so-called vampires have been responsible for the deaths of several persons, by sucking their blood, I have been commissioned by an Honourable Supreme Commander to throw some light on this question."[34]

One of the most startling stories that came to light in Flückinger's report concerned Arnold Paole, a former

Dead Men Returned from the Tomb

French Bible scholar of the Benedictine order Dom Augustine Calmet wrote several books on angels, demons, ghosts, and vampires. The preface to his 1746 book *Essays on the appearances of the angels, the demons and the spirits, and on the ghosts and vampires of Hungary, of Bohemia, of Moravia and Silesia* describes the situation in eastern Europe:

> In this age, a new scene presents itself to our eyes; . . . men, it is said, who have been dead for several months, come back to earth, talk, walk, infest villages, ill use both men and beasts, suck the blood of their near relations, destroy their health, and finally cause their death; so that people can only save themselves from their dangerous visits and their hauntings, by exhuming them, impaling them, cutting off their heads, tearing out their hearts, or burning them. These are called by the name of oupires or vampires, that is to say, leeches; and such particulars are related of them . . . that one can hardly refuse to credit the belief which is held . . . that they come out of their tombs, and produce those effects which are proclaimed of them.

Augustine Calmet, *Essays on the appearances of the angels, the demons and the spirits, and on the ghosts and vampires of Hungary, of Bohemia, of Moravia and Silesia*. London: Richard Bentley, 1850, p. 2.

soldier who lived in Medvegia, north of Belgrade. Paole was described as easygoing and honest, but he had a gloomy personality. After he married in 1727, he told his new wife that his problems began on the battlefield two years earlier when he was bitten by a vampire. After the attack, Paole followed the bloodsucker back to its grave and killed it by driving a stake through its heart. Aware that he might become a vampire himself, Paole tried some common folk remedies to prevent vampirism. He ate dirt taken from the vampire's grave and bathed himself in the creature's blood.

Still haunted by the vampire violence, Paole returned home and bought a farm. However, he fell from a hay wagon, broke his neck, and died shortly after his marriage. About three weeks later, four townsfolk reported that they saw Paole wandering at night. The witnesses all perished shortly after the vision. Alarmed villagers demanded that the local military administrator exhume Paole. When he was dug up, according to Flückinger, they saw his "flesh was not decomposed, his eyes were filled with fresh blood which also flowed from his ears and nose, soiling his shirt and funeral shroud. His fingernails and toenails had dropped off, as had his skin, and others had grown through in their place, from which it was concluded that he was an arch-vampire."[35] A stake was driven through Paole's heart, and his mouth emitted a piercing scream as this was done. In keeping with regional tradition, the body was burned the same day.

Return of the Vampire

Although Paole was disposed of, the vampire contagion he had released upon the people was said to have continued for years. While the original 4 victims of the arch-vampire were exhumed, staked, and burned, Paole was also believed to have drunk the blood of local cows. An unknown number of people ate the meat of the cattle, and these animals were blamed for an infestation that later shook the region. It began in December 1731 when a 50-year-old woman named Miliza began screaming in the middle of the night. She claimed she had been touched on the neck by a man who had been dead 9 weeks. Miliza, who had been in perfect health, became weaker and weaker and died within 4 days. In the immediate aftermath, the vampire epidemic struck the young and very young.

Among the victims who followed Miliza into the grave were a 14-year-old boy named Milloi, a 15-year-old boy named Joachim, and a 2-week-old baby named Petter. A 20-year-old woman named Stanno was also afflicted, as was her week-old child. This was followed by the death of a 9-year-old boy named Wutschiza. Before the vampire plague ended in January 1732, a total of 17 victims, most of under the age of 20, had died under similar circumstances. The epidemic was only stopped when authorities "ordered the heads of all these vampires to be cut off by some wandering gypsies."[36] Their bodies were burned and their ashes cast into the River Moravia.

Emperor Charles believed the vampire investigation would calm fears by exposing the twisted tales as fantasy and rumor. However, Flückinger's report had the opposite effect. It was read by dozens of authors who wrote about Paole and his victims. By the mid-1730s the Moravian case was a public sensation throughout Europe. In France, even the famed philosophers Voltaire and Jean-Jacques Rousseau wrote treatises about vampires, comparing them to corrupt church officials, bankers, and kings. Scientists offered their own explanations for the phenomena of vampirism. Some believed that certain types of soil prevented decomposition, making the dead appear to be alive. Another theory stated that unconscious people were being accidentally buried alive. When they awoke in the grave, they chewed at their shrouds and clawed at the dirt in an attempt to escape their nightmarish situation. It was also said that the screaming of the corpse commonly heard when a stake was driven through its heart was caused by air being suddenly forced from the body.

Whatever the theories of scientists and philosophers, people in rural villages were terrified as rumors of vampire attacks spread through Serbia, Prussia, Poland, and Romania. Many of these stories were fueled by ancient, and often bizarre, beliefs that were deeply ingrained within the populace.

Vampire Characteristics

In Bulgaria people believed that vampires possessed only one nostril, making them easy to spot. In parts of Poland it was thought that a vampire had a long, pointed tongue, like a bee stinger, used to pierce its victims. And the vampire's palms were said to be covered with a soft, downy hair. According to Montague Summers, "the nails are always curved and crooked, often well-nigh the length of a great bird's claw, the [area underneath the nails] dirty and foul with clots and gouts of black blood."[37]

Folktales often described the horrible, fetid stench of the vampire's ice-cold breath. One case widely reported in the seventeenth century concerned 60-year-old Johannes Cuntius, from Pentsch, Silesia. Cuntius led a life that was so evil he turned into a vampire after a horse killed him with a kick to the head.

The story of Cuntius was first described by religious scholar Henry More. In his book *An Antidote Against Atheism*, More described how Cuntius used his stinking breath to sicken the parson of Pentsch Parish:

One evening, when this [parson] was sitting with his wife and Children about him, exercising himself in Musick . . . a most grievous stink arose suddenly. . . . [The smell] encreased, and became above all measure pestilently noisome [disgusting] insomuch that he was forced to go up to his [bed] chamber. He and his Wife had not been in bed an hour, but they find the same stink in the bedchamber; of which, while they are complaining one to another out steps the Spectre [Cuntius] from the Wall, and creeping to his bedside, breathes upon him an exceeding cold breath, of so intolerable stinking and malignant a scent, as is beyond all imagination and expression. Here upon the Theologer, good soul, grew very ill, and was fain to keep his bed, his face, belly, and guts swelling as if he had been poysoned; whence he was also troubled with a difficulty of breathing, and with a putrid inflammation of his eyes.[38]

Tales of virulent breath were also found in Prussia. Summers recounts one story in which a female vampire "was being lifted by [an executioner] on to the pile of wood prepared for her burning and [she] said: 'I will pay you,' and blew into his face. And he was at once afflicted with a horrible leprosy all over his body and did not survive many days."[39]

Vampire Slayers

In many rural parts of Europe it was believed that people would become vampires if they were born with teeth or with deformities, such as a wine-colored birthmark on the face or a twisted, animal-like limb. It was also thought that some were born to hunt and kill vampires. These people had supernatural powers and strength because of their time of birth. For example, it was believed that anyone born on the Saturday before Easter was naturally empowered to be a vampire slayer. Those born on the days between Christmas and New Year's Day, known as the Unclean Days in Moldova and Russia, could also become a vampire hunter, called a *såbotnik.* These slayers could not only detect vampires hiding in the deep forests, but could kill all manner of unclean spirits that haunted the living. In Romani, or Gypsy, tradition, vampire hunters are called *dhampires*, literally "vampire's sons." These are the children of male vampires and mortal females. The half-vampire spawn are common in Gypsy folklore since male vampires are seen as irresistible to women and said to produce many offspring.

Wherever they came from, vampire hunters used special techniques when confronting their prey. Slayers in Bulgaria, called *vampirdzia*, filled their mouths with poison herbs that allowed them to see invisible or shape-shifting animal vampires. When a vampire was detected, the *vampirdzia* could hypnotize the creature by playing a flute or drum. In this way the slayer could lure his prey, like the Pied Piper, into a rushing river or huge bonfire.

Vampirdzias might also trap their prey in a jug or bottle filled with a few spoonfuls of animal blood. To entice the vampire to crawl into the bottle, the slayer chased it relentlessly until the creature was extremely weak and hungry. Starvation would force the creature into the bottle to eat the blood. The hunter then shoved a cork into the bottle, trapping the vampire inside, and threw it into a blazing fire.

With their supernatural powers, slayers were in high demand during the eighteenth-century vampire epidemics.

Widely respected, they were called in to help peasants cope with local vampire outbreaks. When vampires were sufficiently banished from a region, the vampire slayers were richly rewarded with money, gold, jewelry, cattle, and other gifts contributed by a grateful populace.

Illiterate Farmers

Between the 1720s and 1750s, vampire slayers were very busy. Epidemics were reported in eastern Prussia, Hungary, Wallachia, and Russia. However, an outbreak in Moravia in 1755 reached the highest levels of the Austrian government. Fearful

Vampire slayers relied on a variety of tools as can be seen in this early nineteenth-century vampire-killing kit from England. It contains a pistol, silver bullets, a cross, and vials of herbs and potions to ward off the undead.

peasants in the Silesia region began invading graveyards and exhuming corpses of suspected vampires, including those of women and children. The bodies were handed over to executioners, who were ordered to kill the deceased again. News of one such case, concerning a woman in the town of Hermersdorf, alarmed Austrian empress Maria Theresa. The case is described by Hungarian historian Gábor Klaniczay:

> [The] corpse of Rosina Polakin, deceased a few months previously, was exhumed by municipal decision, because people were complaining that she was a vampire and had attacked them at night. Her body was found in good condition (as befits vampires) . . . with blood still present in the veins. According to local custom, the poor family of the deceased was forced to drag the corpse, by means of a hook attached to a rope, through an opening made in the wall of the graveyard, to be beheaded and burnt outside.[40]

Upon hearing the story, the empress dispatched her personal physician, Gerard van Swieten, to Silesia to investigate. Like many educated people of his day, Van Swieten was concerned that peasants who were crazed with vampire mania might be a danger to cultural advancement. Van Swieten wanted to end the epidemic and replace widespread ignorance and superstition with knowledge and reason. As folklorist Bruce A. McClelland writes, "No longer would the imaginings of illiterate farmers or herders in the mountain villages command the attention of what was now properly devoted to the projects of science and technology."[41]

Silliness and Ignorance

Van Swieten investigated the vampire epidemic for several years. He concluded that the entire plague of fear was brought about by "the inclination of the stupid and vulgar crowd towards superstition."[42] Stories of corpses squirting gallons of blood were exaggerated, he said, and he provided one such example to back up his findings:

> One of the vampires "executed" was said to have been swollen with blood, since the executioner, a thoroughly reliable man, no doubt, in matters concerning his trade, claimed that when he cut up bodies, which were sentenced to be burned, a great quantity of blood gushed forth. Nevertheless, he afterwards agreed that this great quantity was about a spoonful—and this is a very different matter.[43]

Even with such evidence, Van Swieten felt compelled to provide scientific explanations for blood-engorged corpses. He noted that he had himself helped exhume corpses, to make room for new bodies in crowded graveyards. During this work the doctor says he observed that about 1 out of every 30 corpses, some buried as long as 15 years, were not decayed. "The contents of the grave are removed, and sometimes whole corpses are encountered rather than putrefied ones, but they are . . . of brownish hue, and the flesh is very toasted. . . . I therefore conclude that a corpse can remain incorrupt for several years, without there being some supernatural cause."[44]

Van Swieten's report resulted in Maria Theresa issuing the 1766 decree called "The Imperial and Royal Law Designed to Uproot Superstition and to Promote the Rational Judgment of Crimes Involving Magic and Sorcery." The law required

A Great Leech Engorged to Bursting

In the classic book *The Vampire: His Kith and Kin*, occult research-er Montague Summers described the physical traits by which a vampire could be recognized in eighteenth-century Europe:

> Vampire is generally described as being exceedingly gaunt and lean with a hideous countenance and eyes wherein glinting the red fire of perdition [Hell]. When, however, he has satiated his lust for warm human blood his body becomes horribly puffed and bloated, as though he were some great leech gorged and replete to bursting. Cold as ice, or it may be fevered and burning as a hot coal, the skin is deathly pale, but the lips are very full and rich, blub and red; the teeth white and gleaming, and the canine teeth wherewith he bites deep into the neck of his prey to suck thence the vital streams which re-animate his body and invigorate all his forces appear notably sharp and pointed. Often his mouth curls back in a vulpine [foxlike] snarl which bares these fangs, a gaping mouth and gleaming teeth. . . . And so in many districts the hare-lipped are avoided as being certainly vampires.

Montague Summers, *The Vampire: His Kith and Kin*. Hyde Park, NY: HP University Books, 1960, p. 179.

judges to consult with scientists and doctors before ruling on cases involving witches or vampires. Those who fraudulently reported vampire cases were to be fined. People with mental or physical illnesses, often mistaken for vampires, were to be hospitalized. While it remained a crime to be a vampire, only the empress could decide upon the punishment. The language of the decree was attributed to Van Swieten, who spelled out the intellectual foundations of the law:

> Silliness and ignorance, which gave rise to simple minded amazement and superstitious practices, have finally led to a situation in which gullibility has gained ground everywhere among the people, who have become incapable of distinguishing reality from illusion. Any event which has seemed to them hard to explain (although caused merely by accident [or] science), has been ascribed to the activities of [vampires] and witches. . . . And these fancies about the vicious herd of [monsters] have been transmitted from one generation to the next. The children are infected from the cradle by terrible fairytales. This craze has spread more and more widely.[45]

While the Austrian edict largely brought an end to vampire hysteria, there were more outbreaks in Wallachia and Russia in 1772. By that time, despite official condemnation, the centuries-old conjecture and rumor surrounding vampires was embedded in popular culture. Many of those who lived through that era could hardly deny the existence of bloodsucking monsters among the people. The vampire epidemic was just as real to those terrified peasants as the black plague, and oftentimes just as deadly.

Chapter 4

Literature Transforms Lore

During the eighteenth century vampires were thought of as repulsive animated corpses that rose from their graves. They were horrifying not only because they were bloodsucking monsters but because they were often well-known members of the community before they died. However, at the beginning of the 1800s, vampire lore was adapted for a changing world.

In the growing cities of Germany, England, and France, poets, writers, and playwrights rewrote ancient vampire tales to create creatures that were different in appearance and demeanor. Nineteenth-century vampires did not appear as zombie-like creatures with flesh hanging off their foul bodies but instead were portrayed as wealthy, well-read, and worldly. As a result of this literary transformation, vampire legend and lore also changed. For example, today it is widely believed that a vampire cannot see its reflection in the mirror. While many think this is part of ancient vampire legends, the concept originated with Bram Stoker's *Dracula* in the late 1890s.

Strange as It Sounds...

Some say Irish writer Bram Stoker derived the word Dracula from the Irish phrase "Droch Ola," which means "bad blood."

Vampire characters like Dracula brought about changes in accepted beliefs, and little by little, the lore surrounding vampires changed too. While it may seem odd that storybook bloodsuckers have influenced legend and lore, many vampire beliefs from the 1600s and 1700s were based on written reports in books, newspapers, and pamphlets. Some historians believe these ancient accounts were nothing more than compilations of rumors, hearsay, and hoaxes—in other words, fiction.

The Gothic Makeover

Some of the first changes occurred during the romantic movement of the late eighteenth century in the area that is now Germany. During this time writers incorporated fears of the unknown into their works to invoke feelings of awe, foreboding, dreamlike wonder, and Gothic horror. And vampires fit perfectly with moody, melancholy romantic literature. Commenting on this trend, the most famous author of the era, Johann Wolfgang von Goethe, referred to his colleagues as "graveyard Romantics" who had a "lust for bizarre and atrocious . . . devils, witches, and vampires."[46]

While Goethe was critical of romantics, he too wrote about devils, witches, and vampires. In 1797 Goethe wrote a poem about vampires called "The Bride of Corinth." His poem was inspired by ancient Greek tales of beautiful vampire women who sap the lifeblood of virile young men. In the poem a woman returns from the dead to reunite with her fiancé. The bride declares:

> From my grave to wander I am forc'd,
> Still to seek The Good's long-severed link,
> Still to love the bridegroom I have lost,
> And the life-blood of his heart to drink.[47]

Tales of Gothic Horror

The term *gothic* is often used alongside *romantic* to describe vampire literature and other horror stories. The word *gothic* was originally used to describe German architecture from the sixteenth century. Author Horace Walpole was fascinated with Gothic architecture. In 1763 Walpole wrote a ghost story called *Castle at Otranto*. Because it was set in a crumbling castle built in the Gothic era, English readers called the story a "gothick" novel. Walpole's preface to *Castle at Otranto* says his story contains "miracles, visions, necromancy, dreams, and other preternatural events." *Castle at Otranto* became a best seller and created a nightmarish vision of the Gothic era that emphasized the grisly, grotesque, and fantastic. Writers of vampires tales, such as Lord Byron, John Polidori, and Anne Rice, were inspired by Walpole, and gothic horror stories have remained popular for more than 250 years.

Horace Walpole, "Reviews of the Castle of Otranto by Horace Walpole," Project Gutenberg, August 12, 2005. www.gutenberg.org.

"The Warm, Purple Tide of Life"

Goethe was one of the most respected authors of his day. He undoubtedly inspired German writer Johann Ludwig Tieck, who wrote "Wake Not the Dead," one of the first fictional stories about vampires, published around 1800. "Wake Not the Dead" is a Gothic horror story in which love for a vampire leads the main character to suffer and die. This theme has long been a part of vampire lore and remains so in countless stories about vampire love today.

As "Wake Not the Dead" begins, Walter and Brunhilda are described as a married couple deeply in love. They are torn apart when Brunhilda suddenly dies. As Walter grieves deeply for his lost love, a sorcerer comes to him, offering to bring his wife back to the world of the living. But even as the wizard agrees to reanimate Brunhilda, he tells Walter, "I warn thee . . . wake not the dead—let her rest."[48]

Lovesick Walter cannot be convinced and begs the sorcerer to bring his love back. The magician casts a spell over Brunhilda's grave, causing a great storm to erupt. The ground opens up, and worms crawling over Brunhilda's body arise and disappear into the heavens in a column of fire. Brunhilda awakens after the sorcerer pours life-giving human blood upon her from a human skull. She bursts forth from her grave, and the lovers embrace. Soon they are on their way to Walter's castle to live again as husband and wife.

Walter is blindly in love, but the servants at the castle are not fooled. They live in what Tieck describes as an "abode of horror" because Brunhilda needs blood to survive:

> It was necessary that a magic draught should animate the dull current in her veins and awaken her to the glow of life and the flame of

love—a potion of abomination—one not even to be named without a curse—human blood, imbibed whilst yet warm, from the veins of youth. This was the hellish drink for which she thirsted. Whenever she beheld some innocent child . . . she would suck from [its] bosom the warm, purple tide of life.[49]

Dozens of local children sickened and died before Brunhilda affixed her bloodthirsty lips to Walter. Only then did Walter realize he was in love with what he calls a creature of blood. With his sense returned to him, Walter takes a sharp dagger and stabs Brunhilda as she sleeps. After Brunhilda is killed, Walter meets another beautiful woman who looks remarkably like her. After a short courtship they are married, but as they are about to spend their first night together, Tieck writes, "Oh! horror! scarcely had he clasped her in his arms ere she transformed herself into a monstrous serpent, which entwining him in its horrid folds, crushed him to death . . . [while] a voice exclaimed aloud—'Wake not the dead!'"[50]

The Vampyre

Tieck wrote several short stories using fantastic themes. And the literature of Tieck and Goethe provided inspiration to romantic writers in England such as Lord George Byron, who explored the subject of vampirism in his 1813 poem "The Gaiour." The poem is based on Greek vampires who return from the graves to feed on their families. Byron describes a curse to be visited upon the gaiour, or nonbeliever:

But first, on earth as vampire sent,
Thy corpse shall from its tomb be rent:

Then ghastly haunt thy native place,
And suck the blood of all thy race;
There from thy daughter, sister, wife,
At midnight drain the stream of life.[51]

"The Gaiour" was Byron's only work about vampires, but he remained intensely interested in supernatural stories. In 1816 Byron hosted a gathering at a villa in Geneva, Switzerland, attended by other romantic writers, including Percy Shelley, Mary Shelley, and Byron's personal physician, John Polidori, a native of Italy. On June 15, as thunder, lightning, and violent rain rocked the villa, Byron challenged the authors to write unique and frightening ghost stories. That night Mary Shelley began work on her classic horror story, *Frankenstein, or the Modern Prometheus*, which describes a doctor who builds a monster from body parts stolen from the graveyard. While *Frankenstein* was the most famous story to emerge that night, Byron's challenge also resulted in *The Vampyre*, by Polidori. This was the first vampire story written in English, and as horror scholar David Skal writes, *The Vampyre* is "one of the most imitated and influential horror stories ever published."[52]

The main character in *The Vampyre*, Lord Ruthven, is described by Polidori as a mysterious nobleman "with a dead grey eye"[53] often seen at London's high society events. As Polidori writes, Ruthven's "peculiarities caused him to be invited to every house; all wished to see him. . . . In spite of the deadly hue of his face . . . many of the female hunters after notoriety attempted to win his attentions, and gain, at least, some marks of what they might term affection."[54]

Although Ruthven is a womanizer and compulsive gambler, a wealthy young man named Aubrey is fascinated with him. The two men become friends and travel to Rome. However, they have a falling out, and Aubrey travels to Greece alone. There Aubrey become infatuated with Ianthe, a beautiful innkeeper's daughter who tells him about vampires living in the region who feed upon the lifeblood of women and children. Aubrey's blood runs cold when he realizes that the local vampires sounds a lot like Ruthven, who soon arrives on the scene.

One twilight while walking in a dark, tangled forest, Aubrey and Ianthe are attacked by a vampire. The young woman is killed, and Aubrey is seriously wounded. However, Ruthven, who is not suspected of Ianthe's murder, compassionately nurses Aubrey back to health, and the two men travel together once again. But they are soon attacked by highway bandits, and Ruthven is mortally wounded. As he lay dying, he impels Aubrey: "Swear by all your soul reveres, by all your nature fears, swear that for a year and a day you will not impart your knowledge of [me] to any living being in any way, whatever may happen, or whatever you may see."[55]

The frightened Aubrey swears not to mention Ruthven for a year and a day and returns to London. Soon after, Aubrey is attending a party when he feels someone grip his arm. He is shocked to see Ruthven, who reminds him of his oath. Because of this promise Aubrey has a nervous breakdown when his only living relative, a sister called Miss Aubrey, is seduced by Ruthven. Aubrey's sister and Ruthven set a date for their marriage on the day the oath ends. The night before the wedding, Aubrey tries to warn his sister, but he dies before he can complete a letter telling her of Ruthven's true nature. Ruthven marries Miss Aubrey and kills her on their wedding night. As Polidori reveals in the last line, "Lord Ruthven had disappeared, and Aubrey's sister had glutted the thirst of a VAMPYRE!"[56]

Million- and Billion-Dollar Vampires

Vampires are often described as wealthy aristocrats, and there is little doubt that vampire stories have brought incredible riches to writers and Hollywood producers. According to the movie business site Box Office Mojo, vampire films have earned $1.3 billion since 1978. Vampires have been extremely popular on TV as well. *Buffy the Vampire Slayer*, which first aired in 1997, drew nearly 4 million viewers every week. In 2008 and 2009 the cable giant HBO was attracting about 7 million viewers per week with the vampire series *True Blood*.

Oftentimes TV and movie vampires first appear in print, and over 3,000 books about bloodsuckers were published between 2000 and 2009. More than 500 such books were published in 2008 alone. Of these, Stephenie Meyer's Twilight series was the biggest hit, selling 27.5 million copies. The first of the Twilight films earned $380 million at the box office in 2008.

The Vampire Takes the Stage

Like Aubrey and Ruthven, Polidori and Byron had a stormy relationship. And it was well known that Polidori modeled Lord Ruthven after the famous Lord Byron, whose public persona was that of a womanizer and gambler. In an added twist to the story, Polidori's tale was published without his permission in London in the *New Monthly Magazine* in April 1819. The magazine, hoping to boost sales, called the story *The Vampyre: A Tale by Lord Byron.* Byron tried to distance himself from the controversy, saying, "I have a personal dislike to Vampires, and the little acquaintance I have with them would by no means induce me to reveal their secrets."[57] However, Goethe described the story as one of Byron's finest accomplishments, permanently cementing Lord Byron's connection to *The Vampyre.*

Polidori did not receive credit for his story until after his death at the age 26 in 1821. But Ruthven took on a life of his own. *The Vampyre* was adapted for at least 4 theatrical productions in 1820 alone. In England Ruthven appeared in the English play *The Vampire, or The Bride of the Isles.* The French version of the play, *Le Vampire,* created a vampire craze that swept through Paris. As Montague Summers writes, "All Paris flocked to see *Le Vampire,* and nightly [the theater] was packed to the doors."[58]

Le Vampire made a star out of the wicked gentleman vampire Ruthven. Discussing the character's contribution to modern vampire lore, literary scholar Leonard Wolf wrote in 1975 that "Polidori gave us the prototypical vampire . . . that is to say, as a nobleman, aloof, brilliant, chilling, fascinating to women, and coolly evil."[59]

Varney the Vampyre

Ruthven was undoubtedly the inspiration for the melodramatic 1845 story *Varney the Vampyre; or, The Feast of Blood*, written by British author James Malcolm Rymer. The tale first appeared in 220 installments in short pamphlets released weekly. The booklets were called penny dreadfuls because of their cheap price and gruesome content. A year after the series was finished in 1847, *Varney the Vampyre* was published in an 868-page book, making it by far the longest vampire story to date.

Varney the Vampyre concerns a reanimated aristocrat, Sir Varney, who is portrayed as a creepy Gothic bloodsucker. According to Rymer, Varney has long, fearsome fangs and fingernails, hypnotic powers, and eyes that glow "like polished tin."[60] Varney hunts his innocent victims in spooky locations as thunder, lightning, rainstorms, and dark nights are expressed in great detail to create an atmosphere of dread. A typical passage describes Varney attacking a young woman, "her bosom heaves, and her limbs tremble, yet she cannot withdraw her eyes from that marble-looking face. . . . With a plunge he seizes her neck in his fang-like teeth—a gush of blood, and a hideous sucking noise follows. The girl has swooned, and the vampire is at his hideous repast!"[61]

Despite his horrid deeds, Varney often expresses familiar human emotions. He loathes his condition and is troubled by his ceaseless quest for the blood of young women. This elicits a sense of empathy for Varney, whose thwarted attacks are often sadly disastrous. The vampire is chased repeatedly, and throughout the long story he is shot, hung, and stabbed with a wooden stake. However, Varney's superhuman powers prevent him from dying, and he can heal his wounds by bathing in moonlight. In the end, however, Varney can no longer tolerate his horrid life, and he commits suicide by throwing himself into the molten lava of Mount Vesuvius in Italy.

While very popular at the time, critics complain that the melodramatic tale of *Varney the Vampyre* is often muddled and difficult to follow. However, the story was one of the most popular penny dreadfuls of the day and, as such, influenced later works of fiction revolving around vampires. Varney was the first vampire to be portrayed in a sympathetic light, an influence that can still be seen today. Nearly every story written in the years that followed featured a conflicted vampire with a melancholy personality who could mesmerize his victims before using his sharp fangs to drain the life force from their bodies.

The Countess Carmilla

Varney the Vampyre influenced Irish author Joseph Sheridan Le Fanu when he wrote *Carmilla* in 1872. Although the vampire Carmilla is a beautiful woman, like Varney she is the incarnation of a wealthy aristocrat.

Carmilla is narrated by an innocent young woman named Laura, who inherits a castle in the Styria region of Austria, where she meets Carmilla. The two young women become friends, but Carmilla inspires in Laura "a vague sense of fear and disgust."[62] The fears are not unfounded, as Carmilla is revealed to be the reanimated body of the Countess Millarca, who died in the 1600s. Laura falls ill with a mysterious ailment traced to Carmilla, who disappears. The story becomes a race against time to find the female vampire and kill her so that Laura may be saved. When Millarca's body is finally located, Le Fanu's description strongly resembles eyewitness accounts written during eighteenth-century vampire epidemics:

[The countess's] eyes were open; no cadaverous smell exhaled from the coffin. . . . The limbs were perfectly flexible, the flesh elastic, and the leaden coffins floated with blood, in which to a depth of seven inches, the body lay immersed. Here then, were all the admitted signs and proofs of vampirism. The body, therefore, in accordance with the ancient practice, was raised, and a sharp stake driven through the heart of the vampire, who uttered a piercing shriek at the moment.[63]

The Cruel, Cunning Count Dracula

Carmilla was not a big seller when it was first published in Ireland. However, Irish writer Bram Stoker acknowledged that *Carmilla* inspired him in 1890 when be began writing *Dracula*, the most famous vampire tale in history. *Dracula* features several prominent female vampires, and like Le Fanu, Stoker drew upon ancient European history to give his story a solid foundation.

The vampire Count Dracula in Stoker's book is named after the infamous Transylvanian mass murderer Vlad Dracula III, the Impaler. Stoker never actually visited Transylvania but read a brief description of Dracula's bloody exploits in *Account of the Principalities of Wallachia and Moldavia*, a book written by British diplomat William Wilkinson in 1820. Perhaps the passage of the book that inspired Stoker to name his character Dracula comes from Wilkinson's translation of the name: "DRACULA in the Wallachian language means Devil. The Wallachians . . . used to give this as a surname to any person who rendered himself conspicuous either by

courage, cruel actions, or cunning."[64]

Courageous, cruel, and cunning accurately describes Stoker's Dracula who, in order to conduct some property acquisitions in England, invites a young British lawyer, John Harker, to his medieval castle in Transylvania. Harker describes Dracula as having massive eyebrows, a bushy mustache, and a mouth that was "rather cruel-looking, with peculiarly sharp white teeth. These protruded over the lips, whose remarkable ruddiness showed astonishing vitality in a man of his years."[65] Harker is nauseated by Dracula's horrible breath, and when the vampire lays a hand on his shoulder, the young Englishman notices sharply pointed fingernails and hairy palms.

Before long, Harker realizes he is the count's prisoner. Harker escapes when Dracula travels to England, where he attacks 19-year-old Lucy Westenra, a wealthy friend of Harker's fiancée, Mina. Lucy falls ill and is examined by scientist and vampire hunter Abraham Van Helsing, a character Stoker likely based on the eighteenth-century vampire investigator Gerard van Swieten. Despite Van Helsing's efforts to save Lucy with blood transfusions, she becomes a vampire and begins preying on children late at night. This prompts Van Helsing and several others to track Lucy down and drive a stake through her heart, a scene described by Stoker: "The Thing in the coffin writhed; and a hideous blood-curdling screech came from the opened red lips. The body shook and quivered and twisted in wild contortions; the sharp white teeth clamped together until the lips were cut, and mouth was smeared with crimson foam."[66]

After Lucy is beheaded, Dracula takes his revenge by biting Mina. The vampire does not kill Mina, but his bite connects her mentally and spiritually with the vampire. Dracula

Strange as It Sounds...

Bram Stoker's Count Dracula was not a creature of the night; he could function during the daytime, although some of his powers were weaker on sunny days.

flees back to his castle in Transylvania, followed by Van Helsing. The story reaches a climax outside Dracula's castle as a battle ensues between Dracula and Van Helsing and his band of rescuers. They cut the vampire's throat with a knife and stab him in the heart. Dracula crumbles into a pile of dust, and his evil spell is lifted from Mina.

Dracula is a literary classic that brings together thousands of years of vampire legend and lore in a story that takes place at the dawn of the twentieth century. Little wonder it was an instant best seller. The Dracula legend continued to grow in 1900 when Stoker, a former theater manager, produced the story on the London stage.

In 1931 the count underwent a Hollywood makeover when he was famously portrayed by actor Bela Lugosi in the film *Dracula*. With his tuxedo, top hat, opera cape, and manners of a suave, Hungarian nobleman, the murderous prince of vampires lost the hairy palms and sharply pointed fingernails. Since that time, Lugosi's sophisticated Dracula has been the model for countless vampires in horror films, comedies, television shows, plays, novels, and even comic books.

Decades of Bloodsuckers

Every decade seemed to have its favorite vampires as tales of bloodsucking monsters continued to multiply in the twentieth century. In the 1960s the exploits of Barnabas Collins, a vampire based on Varney, were featured in the daytime TV soap opera *Dark Shadows*. The 1970s and 1980s were the decades of the vampires Louis and Lestat, the protagonists of Anne Rice's The Vampire Chronicles which began in 1976 with *Interview with the Vampire*. Like gothic authors before her, Rice intertwined ancient legends, lore, and folk beliefs and added fresh twists to create unique vampire characters.

Strange as It Sounds...

Anne Rice, author of *The Vampire Chronicles*, believes vampires are real creatures who must obey the laws of optics and therefore can be seen in mirrors.

In 1994 *Interview* was turned into a blockbuster film starring Brad Pitt, Kirsten Dunst, Antonio Banderas, Christian Slater, and Tom Cruise. And in the late 1990s, vampires were back on the small screen when the TV show *Buffy the Vampire Slayer* gained widespread popularity. In the twenty-first century, interest in vampires continued to grow with the success of Charlaine Harris's Southern Vampire series, which began in 2001. Books in this series about the vampire-loving Sookie Stackhouse were released yearly and turned into the award-winning *True Blood* on HBO in 2008.

Although Sookie Stackhouse was popular, she was soon overshadowed by high school student Bella Swan, the protagonist of the 2005 young adult novel *Twilight*, by Stephenie Meyer. *Twilight* is written from Bella's point of view after she moves from Phoenix to Forks, Washington, where she falls in love with Edward Cullen, a 104-year-old vampire who appears as a permanent 17-year-old.

With its beautiful, sensuous vampire characters who drink animal blood and pose no danger to humans, *Twilight* was an instant best seller. By 2008 the book had sold 17 million copies worldwide, spent over 91 weeks on the *New York Times* best-seller list, and was translated into 37 different languages. Meyer followed with 3 more books in the Twilight series, and all have added new elements to vampire lore. The leading characters in the series have strong, piercing teeth rather than fangs, and unlike Count Dracula, sunlight does not burn them but makes them glitter beautifully. And while Twilight vampires can drink human blood, the lead characters are referred to as vegetarians because they refuse to do so.

For thousands of years, from ancient Africa to Transylvania, from London to Hollywood, vampire lore has found a place in human culture. Perhaps the popularity of vampires

OPPOSITE:
Bela Lugosi's portrayal of Dracula served as a model for countless other vampire characters in books, movies, and television. A movie poster promotes the original film as "The story of the strangest passion the world has ever known!"

Buffy the Vampire Slayer battled vampires, demons, and other evil forces during her six-year run on television. Interest in vampires on the small screen continues with the award-winning HBO show True Blood.

lies in their ability to repel and attract at the same time. Discussing modern vampire tales, William Patrick Day, a professor of cinema and English at Oberlin College, sums up their allure: "Vampires have become a substitute for fairy tales that adults couldn't tell themselves anymore. Vampires are dangerous and sexy and powerful and they have what humans want—immortality."[67]

Source Notes

Introduction: The Kiss That Kills

1. Montague Summers, *The Vampire*. New York: Dorset, 1991, p. vii.
2. Quoted in Montague Summers, *The Vampire: His Kith and Kin*. Hyde Park, NY: HP University Books, 1960, p. 1.

Chapter 1: A History Written in Blood

3. Quoted in Raphael Tenthani, "'Vampires' Strike Malawi Villages," BBC News, December 23, 2002. http://news.bbc.co.uk.
4. Quoted in Summers, *The Vampire: His Kith and Kin*, p. 219.
5. Quoted in J. Gordon Melton, *The Vampire Book*. Detroit: Visible Ink, 1994, p. 5.
6. M.J. Field, *Religion and Medicine of the Ga People*. Oxford, England: Oxford University Press, 1937, pp. 142–43.
7. Field, *Religion and Medicine of the Ga People*, p. 143.
8. Summers, *The Vampire: His Kith and Kin*, p. 265.
9. Summers, *The Vampire: His Kith and Kin*, p. 266.
10. Quoted Hugo G. Nutini and John M. Roberts, *Bloodsucking Witchcraft*. Tucson: University of Arizona Press, 1993, p. 56.

Chapter 2: Spirits Walking by Night

11. Quoted in The Perseus Digital Library, "T. Maccius Plautus, Pseudolus, or The Cheat," 2009. http://old.perseus.tufts.edu.
12. Quoted in Livius, "Flavius Philostratus: The Life of Apollonius," 2009. www.livius.org.
13. Quoted in Livius, "Flavius Philostratus."
14. Quoted in Livius, "Flavius Philostratus."
15. Quoted in Livius, "Flavius Philostratus."
16. Quoted in Keith Whitlock, *The Renaissance in Europe: A Reader*. New Haven, CT: Yale University Press, 2000, p. 331.
17. Quoted in Eli Edward Burriss, "Taboo, Magic, Spirits: A Study of Primitive Elements in Roman Religion," Internet Sacred Texts Archive, 2008. www.sacred-texts.com.
18. Quoted in Summers, *The Vampire*, p. 31.
19. Quoted in Summers, *The Vampire*, p. 31.
20. William of Newburgh, "History of English Affairs, Book 5," Medieval Sourcebook, October 24, 2000. www.fordham.edu.
21. William of Newburgh, "History of English Affairs, Book 5."
22. William of Newburgh, "History of English Affairs, Book 5."
23. William of Newburgh, "History of English Affairs, Book 5."
24. Quoted in Wayne Bartlett and Flavia Idriceanu, *Legends of Blood*. Westport, CT: Praeger, 2007, p. 9.
25. Quoted in Gabriel Ronay, *The Dracula Myth*. New York: W.H. Allen, 1972, p. 22.
26. Quoted in L. Kip Wheeler, "Ghosts and the Renaissance," Carson-Newman College, August 26, 2009. http://web.cn.edu.
27. Rosemary Ellen Guiley, *The Complete Vampire Companion*. New York: Macmillan, p. 9.
28. Guiley, *The Complete Vampire Companion*, p. 9.
29. Bob Curran, *Vampires: A Field Guide to the Creatures That Stalk the Night*. Franklin Lakes, NJ: New Page, 2005, p. 164.
30. Quoted in Sondra London, *True Vampires*. Los Angeles: Feral House, 2004, p. 301.

Chapter 3: A Plague of Vampires

31. Quoted in Ronay, *The Dracula Myth*, p. 24.
32. Augustine Calmet, *The Phantom World:*

The History and Philosophy of Spirits, Apparitions, Etc. London: Richard Bentley, 1850, p. 177.

33. Calmet, *The Phantom World*, p. 181.

34. Quoted in Bartlett and Idriceanu, *Legends of Blood*, p. 14.

35. Quoted in Bartlett and Idriceanu, *Legends of Blood*, p. 14.

36. Quoted in Paul Barber, *Vampires, Burial and Death: Folklore and Reality.* New Haven: Yale University Press, 1988, p. 16.

37. Summers, *The Vampire: His Kith and Kin*, p. 179.

38. Quoted in Summers, *The Vampire: His Kith and Kin*, pp. 179–80.

39. Quoted in Summers, *The Vampire: His Kith and Kin*, p. 180.

40. Gábor Klaniczay, *The Uses of Supernatural Power: The Transformation of Popular Religion in Medieval and Early-Modern Europe.* Princeton: Princeton University Press, 1990, p. 170.

41. Bruce A. McClelland, *Slayers and Their Vampires.* Ann Arbor: University of Michigan Press, 2006, p. 128.

42. Quoted in Darren Oldridge, ed., *The Witchcraft Reader.* New York: Routledge, 2002, p. 388.

43. Quoted in Christopher Frayling, *Vampyres: Lord Byron to Count Dracula.* London: Faber and Faber, 1991, p. 30.

44. Quoted in McClelland, *Slayers and Their Vampires*, p. 141.

45. Quoted in Oldridge, *The Witchcraft Reader*, pp. 388–89.

Chapter 4: Literature Transforms Lore

46. Quoted in Jaroslav Jan Pelikan, *Faust the Theologian.* New Haven, CT: Yale University Press, 1995, pp. 77–78.

47. Johann Wolfgang von Goethe, "The Bride of Corinth," University of Victoria, October 5, 2004. http://web.uvic.ca.

48. Johann Ludwig Tieck, "Wake Not the Dead," SFF Net, 2010. www.sff.net.

49. Johann Ludwig Tieck, "Wake Not the Dead."

50. Johann Ludwig Tieck, "Wake Not the Dead."

51. Lord Byron, "The Giaour," NNTP2HTTP, January 8, 2007. http://alt.nntp2http.com.

52. David J. Skal, *Vampires: Encounters with the Dead.* New York: Black Dog, 2001, p. 37.

53. John Polidori, *The Vampyre*, SFF Net, 2010. www.sff.net.

54. Polidori, *The Vampyre.*

55. Polidori, *The Vampyre.*

56. Polidori, *The Vampyre.*

57. Quoted in Skal, *Vampires*, p. 38.

58. Summers, *The Vampire: His Kith and Kin*, p. 293.

59. Quoted in Bartlett and Idriceanu, *Legends of Blood*, p. 31.

60. Quoted in Leslie S. Klinger, ed., *The New Annotated Dracula.* New York: Norton, 2009, p. xxix.

61. Quoted in Klinger, *The New Annotated Dracula*, p. xxviii.

62. Quoted in Skal, *Vampires*, p. 118.

63. Joseph Sheridan Le Fanu, *Carmilla*, SFF Net, 2010. www.sff.net.

64. Quoted in Bartlett and Idriceanu, *Legends of Blood*, p. 34.

65. Bram Stoker, *Dracula.* Mattituck, NY: Amereon House, 1981, p. 16.

66. Quoted in Klinger, *The New Annotated Dracula*, p. 313.

67. Quoted in Lauren Streib, "Hollywood's Most Powerful Vampires," *Forbes*, August 3, 2009. www.forbes.com.

For Further Exploration

Books

Bob Curran, *Vampires: A Field Guide to the Creatures That Stalk the Night.* Franklin Lakes, NJ: New Page, 2005. One of the few books that explores the rich diversity of vampire beliefs around the world, including India, Sweden, Ireland, Romania, Albania, and Malaysia. Discusses ancient legends, modern lore, and a variety of interesting details about bloodsucking monsters from dozens of cultures.

Stuart A. Kallen, *Vampires.* San Diego: Reference-Point, 2008. This book explores vampires from all ages and cultures, with detailed descriptions of vampire characteristics, weaknesses, and strengths, as well as methods for hunting and killing them.

Leslie S. Klinger, ed., *The New Annotated Dracula.* New York: Norton, 2009. The story of the world's most famous vampire, with analyses, notes, pictures, and definitions throughout the text.

Bruce A. McClelland, *Slayers and Their Vampires: A Cultural History of Killing The Dead.* Ann Arbor: University of Michigan Press, 2006. A thousand years of vampire hunting, trapping, and killing, from the Balkans to Buffy the Vampire Slayer.

Otto Penzler et al., *The Vampire Archives: The Most Complete Volume of Vampire Tales Ever Published.* New York: Vintage, 2009. A volume of 86 vampire tales, poems, and true stories, including classics such as Le Fanu's *Carmilla*, Poe's *Ligeia*, and Stoker's *Dracula's Guest.*

Sally Regan, *The Vampire Book.* New York: DK, 2009. Traces the history of vampire lore in literature, movies, and television and examines folklore about how vampires live, how they avoid capture, and their predatory and romantic relationships with humans.

Web Sites

Anne Rice: The Official Site (www.annerice.com). Official Anne Rice site with news and updates where the author talks to fans about her beliefs, life, books, and vampires characters.

Dracula's Homepage (www.ucs.mun.ca/~emiller). A site hosted by an author and internationally recognized expert on the novel *Dracula*, with many articles about Stoker's life and characters, vampires, Vlad the Impaler, and the Transylvanian Society of Dracula.

Staking Claims: The Vampires of Folklore and Fiction, Committee for Skeptical Inquiry (www.csicop.org/si/show/staking_claims_the_vampires_of_folklore_and_fiction). A well-researched article by Paul Barber about the reality of Vlad Dracula and how myths and legends commonly associated with him have distorted the historical record.

Vampire, The Skeptic's Dictionary (www.skepdic.com/vampires.html). A site maintained by a renowned skeptic who questions the validity of vampire beliefs and provides links to related subjects such as spiritual vampires and transubstantiation.

Vampires (www.vampires.com). This site is a vampire newsmagazine and directory covering popular games, stories, pictures, and books, including *Twilight, True Blood,* and *Vampire Diaries.*

Wake Not the Dead, SFF Net (www.sff.net/people/DoylemacDonald/l_wakeno.htm). This excellent tale, one of the earliest fiction stories about vampires, is posted here, and the SFF home page links readers to Polidori's *Vampyre* and other nineteenth-century vampire stories.

Index